Where Is
Virginia?

Where Is Virginia?

by Jennifer Marino Walters

illustrated by Ted Hammond

Penguin Workshop

To Keith, Matt, Nate, and Lily: This book is for all of you, in honor of the beautiful life we have built in Virginia. You four are my home!—JMW

PENGUIN WORKSHOP
An imprint of Penguin Random House LLC
1745 Broadway, New York, NY 10019
penguinrandomhouse.com

Designed and Produced by Dinardo Design, LLC.

Library of Congress Cataloging-in-Publication Data is available.

First published in the United States of America by Penguin Workshop, 2026

Manufactured in the United States of America
CJKW

ISBN 9798217053346 (paperback)
10 9 8 7 6 5 4 3 2 1

ISBN 9798217053353 (library binding)
10 9 8 7 6 5 4 3 2 1

The authorized representative in the EU for product safety and compliance is Penguin Random House Ireland, Morrison Chambers, 32 Nassau Street, Dublin D02 YH68, Ireland, https://eu-contact.penguin.ie.

Contents

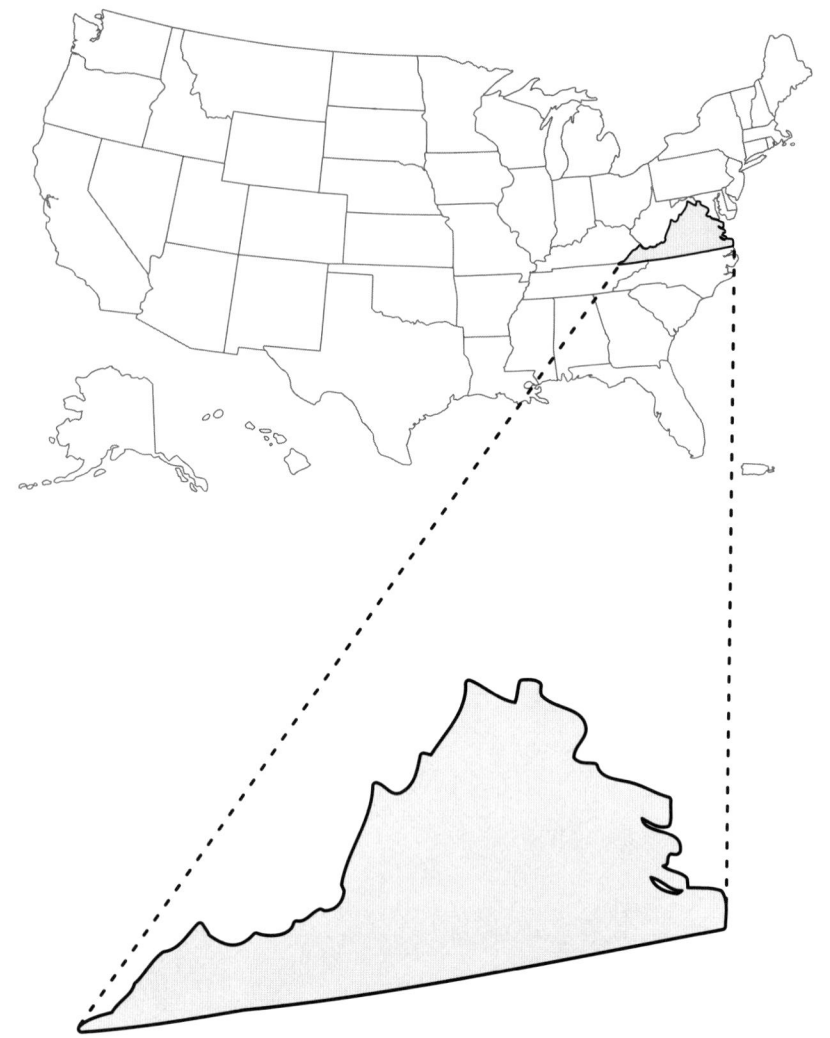

Where Is Virginia?

It was December 1606. More than one hundred men and boys climbed aboard three ships—the *Susan Constant*, the *Godspeed*, and the *Discovery*—and set sail from London. They were headed to a place they believed would bring great opportunity—what would one day be the United States.

King James I of England wanted to set up a colony (an area that would be controlled by England) in America. The English believed they would find gold and silver there and wanted to spread Christianity, their religion. They also hoped to find the Northwest Passage, a sea route westward from the Atlantic Ocean to the Pacific Ocean. This route would enable them to trade with Asia.

King James I did not want to risk losing money if the colony failed. So, he formed the Virginia Company of London. Wealthy men paid money to own parts of the company, which the settlers would use to start the colony. Once the colony was successful, the men would get their money back (plus more).

On April 26, 1607, after four months of sailing, the three ships pulled into what we now call the Chesapeake (say: CHESS-uh-peek) Bay. The settlers chose a marshy peninsula (a piece of land surrounded by water on three sides) as the site of their new colony. They traveled fifty miles up a river from the bay, which they named the James River. They picked a spot they could easily defend if the Spanish (who already had colonies in what is now Florida) attacked.

The colony was called James Fort. Eventually, it was renamed Jamestown. Jamestown became the first permanent English colony in North

America, and it is still a part of the state of
Virginia today.

CHAPTER 1
Virginia's Land, Environment, and Early Peoples

Virginia is in the Southeastern and Mid-Atlantic regions of the United States. It is bordered by Washington, DC, and Maryland to the northeast, the Atlantic Ocean to the southeast, North Carolina and Tennessee to the south, Kentucky to the west, and West Virginia to the northwest. With a population of over 8.8 million, Virginia is the twelfth most populous US state.

Virginia is made up of five different geographical areas. From west to east, they are the Appalachian Plateau, the Valley and Ridge, the Blue Ridge, the Piedmont (say: PEED-mont), and the Coastal Plain.

The Appalachian Plateau, located on the southwestern tip of Virginia, is the smallest of the state's five regions. It is covered in forests and rock.

The Valley and Ridge region is full of ridges (long, narrow hilltops) in the west and valleys in the east. It has many caverns and natural bridges as well as sinkholes. Sinkholes form when soil and rock in the ground are moved by water flowing under the earth's surface. They can appear suddenly as the ground collapses or develop more gradually, or slowly.

The Valley and Ridge region is also home to the Shenandoah (say: shen-en-DOH-uh) Valley and Shenandoah National Park. The famous Appalachian Trail winds through the valley and the national park, offering stunning views. The park also has cascading waterfalls and fields of wildflowers. Skyline Drive, a road that runs through the park, is known as one of the most

scenic drives in North America. It's especially beautiful in fall, when the leaves turn vibrant shades of red, orange, and yellow.

The Blue Ridge region contains the Blue Ridge Mountains, part of the Appalachian Mountains. They are rugged and covered with thick forests. Virginia's highest peak, Mount Rogers, is part of the Blue Ridge. It's 5,729 feet high!

The Piedmont is the state's largest region, full of rolling hills and heavy clay soil. Covering most of central Virginia, the Piedmont stretches from the Blue Ridge in the west to the Fall Line in the east. At the Fall Line, rivers, rapids, and waterfalls cascade off rocks as they flow toward the ocean.

Finally, the Coastal Plain (also known as the Tidewater region) is a low-lying area in eastern Virginia that stretches to the Atlantic Ocean. It's full of swamps, salt marshes, and rivers. The Coastal Plain also includes Virginia's Eastern Shore, part of the Delmarva Peninsula. Most

of Delaware and part of Maryland are also on the Delmarva Peninsula. The Eastern Shore is separated from the rest of Virginia by the Chesapeake Bay. Several of Virginia's rivers—including the Potomac (say: puh-TOH-muck), the York, the James, and the Rappahannock (say: rap-uh-HAN-uck)—flow into the Chesapeake Bay.

The Coastal Plain is home to many of Virginia's beaches, including Virginia Beach. Virginia Beach is not only a popular vacation spot with over thirty-eight miles of coastline but also Virginia's most populous city.

Not all of Virginia is highly populated. Over 62 percent of Virginia is covered in forest. Forests in the Coastal Plain and Piedmont regions have mostly pine trees. The mountain areas have hardwoods such as hickory and oak. Forestry is a big industry in Virginia, with timber (wood that can be used to build things) earning $17 billion each year.

A wide variety of animals live in Virginia. Mammals include black bears, red foxes, beavers, white-tailed deer, brown bats, coyotes, and many more. Cardinals (the state bird), seagulls, bald eagles, red-bellied woodpeckers, and barred owls are some of Virginia's bird species. Barred owls may be territorial, or defensive, around their nests, but they pair up and mate for life. The state is also home to twenty-eight species of frogs and a variety of reptiles, including the poisonous eastern copperhead snake and the legless eastern glass lizard. Even though glass lizards have no legs, they aren't snakes—they have ears and movable eyelids, and snakes don't.

The Chesapeake Bay is the largest marine

life estuary (place where a river flows into the ocean) in the United States and one of the richest estuaries in the world. It's home to more than 3,600 species of plants and animals, such as oysters, clams, blue crabs, and local birds such as the osprey. Beaches, both large and small, dot the Chesapeake Bay area.

Virginia has a temperate (moderate) climate. That means that while it has four distinct seasons, it doesn't usually get extremely hot or extremely cold. The southern and eastern parts of Virginia are warmer than the rest of the state. Virginia receives forty-three inches of precipitation per year on average and sometimes gets large snowfalls.

The first people arrived in the area now known as Virginia about ten to twelve thousand years ago. They were part of the Paleo-Indian culture, and they mainly hunted and fished for their food. Starting around 1000 BCE, the people of the Woodland culture (descendants of the Paleo-Indians) began to grow crops, including corn, beans, and squash. Many of these peoples lived in the coastal parts of what is today eastern Virginia, where they hunted wild birds and fished in the rivers and bays.

By the early 1800s, the largest Indigenous group in Virginia was the Powhatan (say: POW-uh-tan) Confederacy. This was an alliance of some, but not all, of the Indigenous people living in that area. Groups belonging to the Powhatan Confederacy lived in eastern Virginia. They spoke a language known as Virginia Algonquian (say: al-GON-kwee-in) and were united under a powerful ruler named Wahunsenacawh (say: wah-huh-SEN-uh-kuh). He was called Powhatan by the English settlers who arrived while he was leading—the same settlers who would build Jamestown.

CHAPTER 2
The First English Colony

When the English set up Jamestown in 1607, Powhatan's people weren't happy that they were taking over their land. They attacked the colony, and the English fought back. Several people were killed on both sides. The colonists also had trouble finding food, and many died of diseases. By late 1607, only 38 of the original 104 English settlers remained.

In December 1607, Captain John Smith, an English soldier and colonist, traveled in search of food. Powhatan's brother captured him. Smith later wrote that he was brought before Powhatan and was about to be killed when Powhatan's young daughter saved him. Many historians, however, believe they never intended to kill John

Smith. Born with the name Amonute (say: ah-muh-NOOH-tay) and privately called Matoaka (say: mah-toh-AH-kuh), Powhatan's daughter became known by her nickname, Pocahontas, meaning "playful one."

After Smith returned to Jamestown, relations between the Indigenous people and the colonists went back and forth between fighting and friendly trading of food. More settlers (including the colony's first women) continued to arrive from England. Many still died from starvation and disease.

In summer 1609, nine ships carrying over five hundred settlers left England for Jamestown. The ships got caught in a hurricane along the way, and two were lost. Another, the *Sea Venture*, suffered damage from the storm and was shipwrecked on the island of Bermuda with all 150 passengers on board. Some of the ships arrived in Jamestown that August with about three hundred colonists.

The English and the Powhatan Confederacy continued to fight for land and resources. That same year, the Powhatans surrounded Jamestown and trapped the colonists inside with little food. That winter became known as the Starving Time. The settlers were so hungry that they ate anything they could get their hands on—snakes, cats, dogs, horses, mice, and even shoe leather. Many of them starved to death. Others grew so weak that they caught deadly diseases. Over 75 percent of the colonists died that winter.

When the people from the Powhatan Confederacy finally retreated in May 1610, only sixty English colonists remained in Jamestown. Then the *Sea Venture* survivors arrived on two ships they'd built. One of them was a man named John Rolfe, who brought tobacco seeds that he likely got in the Caribbean during the journey. The English found this tobacco to be less bitter than the tobacco grown by Virginia's Indigenous people. Rolfe planted the seeds and soon sent his first crop of tobacco to England. People there loved it, and tobacco quickly became Virginia's most important cash crop.

The colonists also continued to claim land as their own in Virginia. They set up another settlement, Henrico, at a different spot on the James River.

Fighting with Powhatan Confederacy people continued. In April 1613, some colonists kidnapped Pocahontas and brought her to Jamestown. They wanted Powhatan to release several English hostages and return weapons and tools that had been stolen. Powhatan released the hostages, but not the weapons and tools. The English kept Pocahontas.

While in captivity, Pocahontas converted to Christianity and took the English name Rebecca. With Powhatan's consent, she married John Rolfe on April 5, 1614, and they had a

son named Thomas in 1615. But only two years later, Pocahontas became very sick. She died on March 17, 1617.

The details of Pocahontas's conversion to Christianity and marriage to Rolfe remain under debate. One version of the story that was popular with the English was that Pocahontas willingly became a Christian and got married because she fell in love with Rolfe. Many Indigenous and other people believed she did these things only to survive and to protect her people, and some historians now agree.

In any case, the marriage of Pocahontas and Rolfe led to a long period without war between the English and the Powhatan Confederacy. Rolfe continued to improve his tobacco crops. By the end of 1617, twenty thousand pounds of tobacco had been shipped to England. That amount doubled the following year. Twelve years later, 1.5 million pounds of tobacco were grown in

Virginia and sent to England and other countries to be sold.

In 1618, the Virginia Colony authorized a General Assembly for Jamestown. It met for the first time in 1619. The assembly included Virginia's governor and representatives chosen by white, property-owning men. This General Assembly was the first representative government in North America. A representative government is one in which citizens vote for people to speak and make decisions for them. The Virginia General Assembly still meets today.

In August 1619, the first African people— over twenty people who'd been kidnapped from Angola—arrived in Point Comfort, Virginia. They had been on a Portuguese ship that kidnapped and enslaved people, and then they were taken from that ship by the English. Most of them were enslaved by wealthy plantation owners in Point Comfort. Some went to Jamestown. This was the beginning of nearly 250 years of slavery in America.

After more disease, starvation, and fighting with the Powhatan Confederacy in Virginia, King James I took control of the colony away from the Virginia Company. He made Virginia a royal colony under his control. Jamestown was its capital.

The English continued to establish new settlements in Virginia. One of them was a small village called Middle Plantation, founded in 1632 between the York and James Rivers. King William III and Queen Mary II founded the College of William & Mary (W&M) there in 1693. Only Harvard University had been established earlier. Today, W&M is still the second-oldest college in the United States. The Sir Christopher Wren Building is the oldest college building still in use in the country.

In 1699, Virginia's capital moved to Middle

Plantation. The city was renamed Williamsburg after King William III. Williamsburg quickly grew into a center of trade, culture, and government.

Many Scotch Irish people (descendants of Scottish people who settled in Northern Ireland) and German people also moved to Virginia. They came mainly to the Shenandoah Valley where

they could buy fertile land (land that is good for growing things) to set up farms. The English began setting up colonies outside of Virginia, too.

In 1707, England and Scotland joined together to form the Kingdom of Great Britain. By 1732, there were thirteen British colonies in America: Connecticut, Delaware, Georgia,

Maryland, Massachusetts, New Hampshire, New Jersey, New York, North Carolina, Rhode Island, Pennsylvania, South Carolina, and Virginia. The colonies began to rebel against their British rulers. They were unhappy that the British were trying to take more control and make them pay new taxes.

This rebellion led to the American Revolutionary War, which started in 1775. General George Washington, who had been born in Virginia, led the colonial army against the British. The colonies declared independence from Great Britain and formed the United States in 1776. Thomas Jefferson, also from Virginia, wrote the famous Declaration of Independence to mark the occasion. But the war continued.

In 1779, Jefferson became Virginia's second governor. He moved Virginia's capital to Richmond because he believed its inland location (away from the coast) would protect it from British attack. Many Revolutionary War battles took place in Virginia. These include the final battle in Yorktown, where British General Charles Cornwallis surrendered on October 19, 1781. The war officially ended in 1783.

After that, some of the important leaders from the colonies joined together to form the new US government. These men became known as America's Founding Fathers. Several of them were from Virginia, including George Washington, Thomas Jefferson, George Mason, and James Madison. Madison is known as the "Father of the Constitution" because he was its main author. The US Constitution was written in 1787. Virginia was the tenth state to ratify, or approve, it.

CHAPTER 3
Growth and Development

In the decades that followed, Virginia continued to be a leader of the new nation. Four of the first five US presidents were from Virginia: George Washington (1789 to 1797), Thomas Jefferson (1801 to 1809), James Madison (1809 to 1817), and James Monroe (1817 to 1825).

Slavery continued to grow in Virginia and other US states. In fact, these first four US presidents from Virginia were enslavers. In addition to working on plantations, people in Virginia who were enslaved were forced to work as miners, shipbuilders, and more. By 1860, over half a million enslaved people lived in Virginia, making up nearly one-third of the state's population. They were a driving force of the state's economy.

Slavery led to the American Civil War, which began in 1861. Virginia and ten other Southern states seceded (removed themselves) from the Union to form the Confederacy, with Richmond as its capital. More than twenty other states remained in the Union, led by President Abraham Lincoln. The Union wanted to end slavery. The Confederacy wanted slavery to continue.

Most Civil War battles took place in Virginia. They included both the first major battle of the war, the Battle of Bull Run near Manassas (1861), and one of the last battles, the Battle of Appomattox (say: app-oh-MAT-ix) Court House (1865). Confederate Commander Robert E. Lee surrendered to Union Commander Ulysses S. Grant there. That surrender led to the end of the war in 1865. That same year, the Thirteenth Amendment to the US Constitution officially abolished slavery, or made it illegal. Virginia formally rejoined the United States in 1870.

One of the people freed by the Thirteenth Amendment was a nine-year-old boy named Booker T. Washington. He had been born in Virginia. After he and his family were freed, they moved to West Virginia, where he began working in a salt furnace (a place where salty water is heated so that the salt can be removed) and later in a coal mine.

Washington enrolled in the Hampton Normal and Agricultural Institute in Virginia (now Hampton University) in 1872. In 1881, he was chosen to lead a new school, the Tuskegee Normal and Industrial Institute (now Tuskegee University), in Alabama. The school trained African Americans to be teachers and taught them skills such as farming and blacksmithing. Washington believed that training for jobs and gaining economic independence (the ability to make their own money and decide how to spend it) would help Black people get equal rights.

Black people struggled for equal rights across the United States, including in Virginia. Many Southern states passed laws that required segregation (the separation of Black people and white people in public places such as schools and restrooms). Many, including Virginia, also required people to pay poll taxes and take literacy tests to vote, which made it difficult for many Black people to use their rights. In 1924, Virginia passed the Racial Integrity Act, which made it illegal for people of different races to marry each other.

As a response to this inequality, the fight for equal rights grew. This involved many groups and individuals working to get equal rights for all people regardless of race, sex, or religion, and it was led by Black Americans. Change was slow. It wasn't until 1954 that the Supreme Court declared public school segregation illegal. Some counties in Virginia integrated their schools, but many resisted.

Ten years later, the Civil Rights Act of 1964 was passed. This federal law prohibited discrimination based on race, color, religion, sex, and national origin, which included segregation.

The national Voting Rights Act of 1965 banned the poll taxes and literacy tests that had kept many Black people from voting. But interracial marriage was still illegal in sixteen states (mostly in the South), including Virginia.

President Lyndon B. Johnson signs the 1964 Civil Rights Act

Loving v. Virginia

Richard Loving, a white man, and Mildred Jeter, a Black woman—both from Central Point, Virginia—fell in love and got married in June 1958. They married in Washington, DC, because interracial marriage was illegal in Virginia. After their marriage, the Lovings returned home.

In the middle of the night on July 11, 1958, a sheriff woke them up and arrested them. They were sentenced to one year in jail but were told they wouldn't have to go if they left Virginia. So the couple left their home and moved to Washington, DC, where they raised three children.

In 1963, the Lovings got lawyers and began to fight back. Their case went all the way to the US Supreme Court. On June 12, 1967, the Supreme Court ruled in *Loving v. Virginia* that Virginia's interracial marriage law violated the US Constitution. The

ruling also overturned similar laws in fifteen other states. Finally, the ban on interracial marriage was lifted, and the Lovings returned to Virginia.

After schools were integrated and the Civil Rights Act was passed, the suburbs of Virginia grew steadily. This was especially true in Northern Virginia, part of the larger Washington, DC, area. And as Northern Virginia's population increased, so did the area's arts scene.

In 1966, a woman named Catherine Filene Shouse (say: fuh-LEEN SHAUS) donated nearly one hundred acres of farmland in Vienna, Virginia, to the US government. A lover of nature and the arts, Shouse also donated money for the government to build a large amphitheater (a rounded, outdoor space with rising seats like a theater) on the land. The US government designated the land as a national park that would come to be known as Wolf Trap National Park for the Performing Arts. The amphitheater, called the Filene Center, was completed in 1971.

Today, Wolf Trap remains the only national park dedicated to the performing arts. Pop and country music concerts, musicals, operas, dance performances, and more take place there each year at the Filene Center and at The Barns at Wolf Trap, an indoor theater that opened in 1982. Wolf Trap's Children's Theatre-in-the-Woods, open since 1975, shows family-friendly concerts, puppet shows, plays, and more during the summer. It's just one example of how the arts and nature remain a big part of life in Virginia.

Virginia also made history in 1990 when L. Douglas Wilder became the state's governor. Wilder—the grandson of enslaved people and a graduate of segregated public schools in Richmond—was the first elected African American governor in US history. He served as governor until 1994 and later was the mayor of Richmond from 2005 to 2009. Several buildings at colleges and universities in Virginia are named after him.

CHAPTER 4
Today's State

Today, more than one-third of Virginians live in Northern Virginia. Since Northern Virginia makes up only 3 percent of the state's total land area, it's the most crowded part of the state. Northern Virginia is also responsible for over 40 percent of the state's economy.

Many people who live in Northern Virginia work for the federal government. They commute into Washington, DC, by train, bus, or car. A lot of federal employees work at the Pentagon, the headquarters of the US Department of Defense, in Arlington (just across the Potomac River from DC). Open since 1943, the building is called the Pentagon because it has five sides. It's one of the biggest office buildings in the world. The

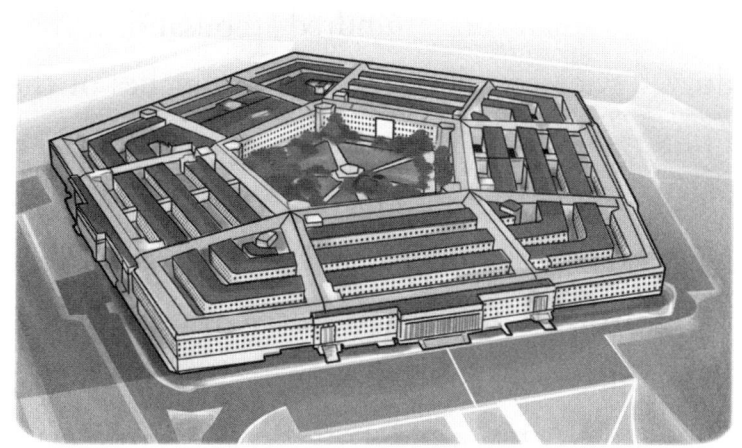

Pentagon has over six million square feet of office space throughout its seven stories. That's more than one hundred football fields of space!

Many software and technology companies also have offices in Northern Virginia. These include huge companies such as Google and Amazon. The headquarters of the Central Intelligence Agency (CIA) are in Northern Virginia. The CIA is responsible for collecting and analyzing (or studying) information that will keep the country safe. Some people who work for the CIA are real-life spies!

More than one hundred thousand active-duty service members from five branches of the military—Army, Navy, Air Force, Marines, and Coast Guard—are stationed in Virginia at various bases. Naval Station Norfolk, open since 1917, is the world's largest naval base. Marine Corps Base Quantico, Joint Base Langley-Eustis (Air Force and Army), and Fort Belvoir (Army) are three other large military bases in the state. And the Wallops Flight Facility on Wallops Island, Virginia, is the only launch site that's owned and operated by the National Aeronautics and Space Administration (NASA).

Many people also visit Arlington National Cemetery in Northern Virginia. Open since 1864, the cemetery serves as the final resting place for over four hundred thousand veterans (including service members from every major American war) and their spouses and children. Visitors can see the grave sites of Presidents John

F. Kennedy and William Howard Taft, astronaut John Glenn, Supreme Court Justice Ruth Bader Ginsburg, and many other famous Americans.

Though agriculture isn't as important in Virginia as it once was, there are still nearly 39,000 farms throughout the state. These farms provide over 380,000 jobs. Corn, wheat, soybeans, apples, and tobacco are some of the state's biggest crops.

The tourism industry is also big in Virginia. With all its history and natural beauty, the state draws millions of visitors each year. Many people visit Virginia to see the famous wild ponies that roam the marshes, forests, and beaches of Chincoteague (say: shing-kuh-TEEG) Island, off the coast of the state, as well as nearby Assateague (say: AS-uh-teeg) Island, part of which is in Virginia (the other part is in Maryland).

Most historians believe the ponies are descendants of horses that were brought to the islands in the early 1700s by settlers who wanted

to avoid livestock taxes. There are over 225 horses on the islands today. About 150 of them are on the Virginia side. Each year in July, people called saltwater cowboys round up the horses from the Virginia side of Assateague and help them swim to Chincoteague. Thousands of people come to watch the event. Once in Chincoteague, the ponies are examined and given medical care if they need it. Then the cowboys mark 150 of them to return to the wild, and the rest are sold.

Eight US presidents have been born in

Virginia, more than any other state: George Washington, Thomas Jefferson, James Madison, James Monroe, William Henry Harrison, John Tyler, Zachary Taylor, and Woodrow Wilson. Six of their homes—Washington's Mount Vernon, Jefferson's Monticello, Madison's Montpelier, Monroe's Highland, Harrison's Berkeley Plantation, and Tyler's Sherwood Forest Plantation—are open to visitors.

Virginia's Historic Triangle in eastern Virginia—Jamestown, Williamsburg, and Yorktown—is another popular tourist spot. Visitors explore Historic Jamestowne—the site of the original Jamestown fort—and the nearby Jamestown Settlement, where historical interpreters demonstrate life in the early colony. They tour Yorktown Battlefield, including the spot where Cornwallis surrendered. And they experience life in colonial America by visiting the historic buildings of Colonial Williamsburg.

Living History

After Virginia's capital moved to Richmond in 1780, Williamsburg was much less busy. Over the next 150 years, it transformed from a bustling city into a quiet college town.

Rev. Dr. William Archer Rutherfoord Goodwin, the former pastor of Williamsburg's church, returned to Williamsburg in 1923. He was alarmed that many of the historic buildings were falling apart. So, he began raising money to save them.

In 1926, John D. Rockefeller Jr., a wealthy New Yorker who was famous for giving money to organizations including libraries and schools, agreed to provide the money to restore Colonial Williamsburg. He and Goodwin began buying the town's buildings. Over the next thirty years or so, workers used pictures and other documents to help them restore or rebuild hundreds of buildings to look just like they did in the 1700s.

Today, Colonial Williamsburg is the world's largest living history museum. Its eighty-nine original buildings and hundreds of reconstructed ones include houses, shops, the courthouse, the governor's palace, and more. Visitors can enter many of these buildings and watch tradespeople—including carpenters, bookbinders, tailors, and others—at work.

Virginia is the most populous state without a major professional sports team. Many Virginians are fans of Washington, DC, teams such as Major League Baseball's Washington Nationals and the National Basketball Association's Washington Wizards. Two DC teams practice in Virginia— the National Hockey League's Washington Capitals in Arlington and the National Football League's Washington Commanders in Ashburn. Fans can watch the Capitals practice for free at MedStar Capitals Iceplex in Arlington.

Golf is popular in Virginia, with many courses in the state. NASCAR holds races on two Virginia racetracks. There are several big ski resorts in Virginia, including Massanutten, Bryce, Wintergreen, and Omni Homestead. Olympic gold medal–winning Virginians include Gabby Douglas, who in 2012 became the first African American to win the gymnastics individual all-around gold, and Noah Lyles, who grew up in

Virginia and won gold in the men's 100-meter race in 2024. In fact, Virginia athletes alone won fourteen medals at the Paris Olympics in 2024!

Virginia is home to more than 150 colleges and universities, such as the University of Virginia, James Madison University, and Virginia Tech. The Virginia Military Institute (VMI) is the oldest state-supported military college in the country.

While people have come from all over to live and work in Virginia, there are still more than one hundred thousand Indigenous peoples living in the state. They are part of eleven state-recognized Indigenous nations, including the Chickahominy (say: chick-uh-HAH-min-ee), Pamunkey, Rappahannock, and more.

Virginia is a place where colonial sites, battlegrounds, and historic places exist alongside modern roads, shops, and restaurants. It's a place where the past and the present come together.

Virginia at a Glance

Statehood: 1788

Nickname: Old Dominion

Abbreviation: VA

State Motto: *Sic semper tyrannis* (Latin for "Thus always to tyrants")

State Tree: Flowering dogwood

Capital: Richmond

Size: 42,775 square miles

Population: Over 8 million

Famous People from Virginia:

Arthur Ashe (tennis champion), Sandra Bullock (actress), Pharrell Williams (singer and music producer), Allen Iverson (former NBA basketball player), Camila Mendes (singer)

Richmond

State flag

State bird
Northern cardinal

State flower
Flowering dogwood

FUN FACT:
The first peanuts commercially grown in the United States were grown in what is now Virginia.

Timeline of Virginia

1607 — Jamestown, the first permanent English settlement in North America, is established

1619 — The Virginia General Assembly, the oldest current law-making body in North America, meets for the first time

1693 — The College of William & Mary opens

1776 — Thomas Jefferson writes the Declaration of Independence

1780 — Richmond becomes the capital of Virginia

1781 — The British surrender in Yorktown, eventually leading to the end of the American Revolutionary War

1861 — Virginia joins the Confederacy

1865 — Confederate General Robert E. Lee surrenders to Union General Ulysses S. Grant at Appomattox Court House

1870 — Virginia rejoins the United States

1917 — Naval Station Norfolk opens

1926 — John D. Rockefeller Jr. agrees to provide money to restore Colonial Williamsburg

1943 — The Pentagon opens in Arlington

1967 — Virginia ends its ban on interracial marriage after the *Loving v. Virginia* case

2024 — Virginia athletes win fourteen medals at the Paris Olympics

Timeline of the World

1608 — French explorer Samuel de Champlain founds the city of Quebec

1620 — Pilgrims arrive in Plymouth Harbor

1707 — The Acts of Union combine England and Scotland into the Kingdom of Great Britain

1789 — The French Revolution begins

1824 — Mexico becomes a republic three years after declaring independence from Spain

1862 — The first paper money is issued in the United States

1892 — Ellis Island opens as a US immigration station

1896 — The first modern Olympic Games take place in Greece

1916 — Congress establishes the National Park Service

1927 — Pilot Charles Lindbergh completes the first transatlantic flight, flying from New York to Paris

1947 — Jackie Robinson plays his first game with the Brooklyn Dodgers, ending segregation in Major League Baseball

1967 — The world's first human heart transplant surgery is performed in South Africa

2024 — *Odysseus* becomes the first American-built spacecraft to land on the moon since 1972

Bibliography

*Books for young readers

*Boehm Jerome, Kate. *Virginia: What's So Great About This State?* Charleston, SC: Arcadia Publishing, 2011.

*Hackett, Jennifer. *Virginia*. A True Book: My United States. New York: Scholastic Inc., 2018.

*Mattern, Joanne. *Historic Williamsburg: A Revolutionary City*. South Egremont, MA: Red Chair Press, 2018.

Websites

Colonial Williamsburg: www.colonialwilliamsburg.org

Historic Jamestowne: www.historicjamestowne.org

Jamestown Settlement and the American Revolution Museum at Yorktown: www.jyfmuseums.org

Mount Vernon: www.mountvernon.org